ESSENTIAL TIPS

Caring for your

DOG

ESSENTIAL TIPS

Caring for your

DOG

Dr. Bruce Fogle DVM, MRCVS

DORLING KINDERSLEY
London • New York • Stuttgart

A DORLING KINDERSLEY BOOK

Editor James Harrison
Art Editor Ann Thompson
Managing Editor Mary-Clare Jerram
Managing Art Editor Amanda Lunn
Production Controller Meryl Silbert

First published in Great Britain in 1995 by
Dorling Kindersley Limited,
9 Henrietta Street, London WC2E 8PS

A CIP catalogue record for this book is available from the British Library

ISBN 07513-0181-7

Computer page make-up by Mark Bracey
Text film output by The Right Type, Great Britain
Reproduced by Bright Arts Ltd
Printed and bound by Graphicom, Italy

ESSENTIAL TIPS

HOW TO CHOOSE A DOG

1 WHY BUY A DOG?

Keeping a dog as a pet is a joy – it will give companionship, amusement, and the incentive to take exercise, as well as becoming the focus for a family's affections. But ownership also means responsibilities for many years ahead: so ask yourself first what you can commit. Have you time to exercise a dog daily? Are you prepared to scoop poop? Are you aware of the long-term costs of dog food, vet care, and kennels, for example?

Show dogs are judged against exacting breed standards

Golden Retrievers are responsive to training and alert, but require plenty of exercise

Bearded Collies make friendly family pets

△ HOUSE PET
A family dog provides constant companionship and affection in the home.

◁ SHOW DOG
Do you want to show your dog? This can become an all-consuming hobby as the dog has to be immaculately groomed and totally trained, with all vaccinations up to date.

Working dogs like
Labrador Retrievers
need more exercise
(and a larger diet)
than equivalent
house dogs

Chihuahuas are
tiny, plucky, and
playful pets

△ COMPANION, OR LAP DOG
Small companion dogs can be a great
comfort, but they need more exercise
than you might expect because they
are active breeds. Their size means
they are less expensive to feed.

△ WORKING DOG
Do you need a trained dog to help you or a
relative with a physical disability? Working
dogs are highly intelligent and eager to serve.
They are also specially trained to be an aid.

GUARD DOG ▷
Breeds like Rottweilers
offer protection and
security. But to own
one you must be
experienced in dog
handling, and be
aware of what the
law requires.

Immensely
powerful,
Rottweilers
are fierce if
aroused

2 WHY BUY A PEDIGREE?

Pedigree breeds come with documentation, just like cars, and there is also plenty of information about their size, feeding, and energy requirements, as well as temperament. Purchase a pedigree from a recognized breeder, and check it has a certificate of its lineage, and a vaccination record.

SAFE IN THE KNOWLEDGE
Do your homework before you buy a pedigree like this Basenji.

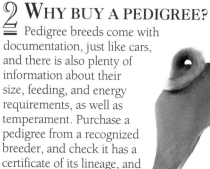

A happy nature is associated with cross-breeds.

△ **CROSS-BRED CHOICE**
A cross-bred dog, like this Jack Russell and Border Terrier cross, is unlikely to develop any of the negative health or temperament aspects associated with its parents' pure breeding.

3 CROSS-BRED OR RANDOM-BRED?

Not everyone can afford a pedigree so you are left with a choice between cross-bred or random-bred dogs. As its name suggests, a cross-bred dog is the offspring of two pure-bred dogs and often combines the better traits of both. Random-bred dogs are further removed from pure-bred dogs; the randomness of their breeding means they are less likely to inherit diseases and disabilities than pure-breds.

◁ **RANDOM-BRED CHOICE**
It can be very difficult to determine how big a random-bred puppy will grow, as it comes from such mixed parentage.

HOW TO CHOOSE A DOG

4 COATS TO CONSIDER

Coat type is a critical consideration when choosing a dog. Some breeds' coats require daily grooming; with others bathing can be a chore, as can keeping moulting hair off furniture.

◁ **LONG & SILKY**
Long-coated dogs, like the Afghan Hound, need daily combing and a regular trim.

△ **SMOOTH COAT**
Smooth, short-haired coats are the easiest to maintain with weekly brushing, as with the Dobermann.

◁ **CURLY COAT**
Non-shedding, curly coats, as on this Kerry Blue Terrier, must be clipped every two months.

△ **WIRY COAT**
The stiff, dense hair of an Airedale Terrier requires regular hand-stripping or clipping.

5 WHICH SEX, MALE OR FEMALE?

Choosing between a male dog or bitch can be difficult, but remember:
- Young unneutered males can be a nuisance when in hypersex mode.
- Bitches go "on heat" twice a year and this demands extra vigilance.
- Owning a bitch means unwanted pregnancies and male dog attention.

11

6 A PERFECT PUPPY?

A dog is for life, and opting for a puppy could mean sharing the next 14 years with your pet. Choose a puppy over eight weeks old.

1 Lift the ear flaps to see if the ear is pink inside, with neither an unpleasant odour nor any sign of crusty or waxy discharge. Such deposits or discharges might indicate ear mites. Check that the ear-flaps hang evenly. Some head and ear shaking is normal, especially after waking.

△ LIFT UP TO CHECK UP
A healthy puppy is happy to be picked up and should feel firm and heavier than you expect. If it is relaxed when lifted, this might indicate an easygoing adult-to-be. Observe the puppy in its litter: this can show you its likely temperament.

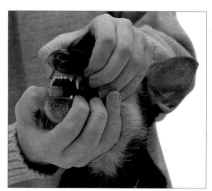

3 To check teeth and gums, gently part the lips. See that the gums and tongue are pink (or mottled with black pigment), and odour-free. Gums should form a clean margin with the teeth. In most breeds (the Boxer is an exception), the teeth should generally meet perfectly in a scissor bite.

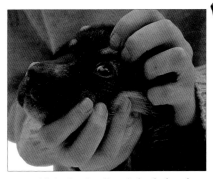

A PUPPY'S FUR SHOULD BE SHINY

2 Hold the head still and check that the eyes are clear, bright, and free from any discharge – stains around the facial hair might indicate the latter. There should be good pigmentation and no sign of redness, squinting, or inflammation. A puppy that paws at its eyes may have an irritation.

4 Check for oily or flaky skin and make sure there are no sores or lumps. The hair should be firm and not come out when you stroke it (healthy fur glistens and only comes out when moulting). Run your hand against the grain of the coat to help you spot any skin defects or parasites.

5 The anal region under the tail should be clean and dry. There should be no inflammation, or sign of diarrhoea, dried faeces, or other discharge from the genitals. Dragging the rear along the floor, or excess licking, can indicate an irritation caused by blocked anal glands.

7 Test before you buy

If you decide to purchase a mature dog, over six months old, do not go just on appearances. Before you take it away, try to test its temperament by seeing if it seems willing to obey and to respond to commands, accepts being touched, is not hand-shy or nervous in any way, and also does not bark at every opportunity.

Gauge a Dog's Response to Training
Will the dog sit on command? If it refuses to sit, tuck it into a sitting position to see how it might then respond to your voice and physical presence.

8 Where to buy

First ask your vet for sources. Animal shelters are another source but the dog may take time to settle down. Look also in your local paper.

9 Tag your dog

In most countries the law on dogs dictates that you must have an identity tag on your dog's collar.

Inside data

Roll Tag
The owner and dog details go on a paper roll inside the tag.

Brass Tag
Practical and designed to last.

10 Vet check

Ask pet-owning friends to recommend a vet. Visit the surgery to see if the place suits your needs and to discuss your dog's vaccinations, diet, worming, and check-ups.

ANNUAL CHECK-UP

FIRST HANDLING

11 CARRYING A PUP

Accustom your puppy, or small dog, to being picked up and carried. Reassure it first, especially a small dog, before trying to pick it up. Aim to hold the animal firmly, but comfortably, and stop it from squirming and paddling. The grasp shown here will prevent it jumping.

CORRECT HOLD FOR PUPPY/SMALL DOG
Place one hand under the small dog's or puppy's forelimbs and chest. Put the other hand around the hind limbs and rump for firm control. Lift your dog in this position.

PUPPY FEELS SAFE AND COMFORTABLE

12 PICKING UP A LARGE DOG

Even large dogs must be lifted occasionally; it is best to teach them this at a young age. Always talk to your dog to reassure it before trying to pick it up. Muzzle it if in any doubt about its temperament. Place one of your arms around the dog's chest and forelimbs, the other around its rump, then lift it up.

1 Bend your knees, draw the dog to your chest, and straighten your back.

2 Lift it up in a secure grip, keeping your back straight. Release if it panics.

15

13 COLLAR CHOICE

Collars are made from leather, rope, or firm, supple meshed nylon. Attach an ID tag to the collar. Puppies should wear collars from eight weeks old, but with some supervision at first.

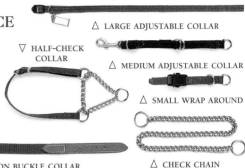

△ LARGE ADJUSTABLE COLLAR

▽ HALF-CHECK COLLAR

△ MEDIUM ADJUSTABLE COLLAR

△ SMALL WRAP AROUND

△ SMALL LEATHER AND NYLON BUCKLE COLLAR

△ CHECK CHAIN

▷ REFLECTIVE COLLAR

▷ LEATHER AND NYLON COLLAR

14 COLLAR IT

Put a puppy's first collar on for short periods each day so it grows used to it. Remove the collar when you cannot supervise the puppy. As the dog grows in size, check the collar size and change as necessary.

1 △ Check the length of the collar around the dog's neck. Make sure it does not catch a long-haired dog's fur.

2 ▷ You should be able to slip two fingers under a well-fitting collar. The collar will not come off if the dog tugs backwards on its lead, but can be slipped off without discomfort if needed.

15 How to choose a lead

With a puppy or new dog, start with
one long training lead for outdoor training, and
a long light houseline with a bolt snap
for indoor control. Also buy one short
lead for first walks and early training.
Do not use leads to punish dogs.

◁ 2 M (6 FT)
COTTON LEAD

△ EXTENSION
LEAD

◁ NYLON CORD
LONG LINE

◁ 6 M (20 FT)
COTTON LEAD

△ STANDARD LEATHER LEAD

16 Help with head halters & harnesses

A head halter is ideal for
a fearful or bold dog and
for one that chews too
much. Made of strong
nylon, it clips onto a lead
via a ring under the dog's jaw. If
the dog pulls or lunges, its own
momentum pulls its head down
and its jaws shut. This is an
alternative to a check chain.

A harness for small dogs
slips over the body and
around the chest. The
lead is attached
over the dog's
back to avoid
collar pressure
on the neck.

△ HEAD HALTER

△ HEAD HALTER ADAPTER

◁ ADJUSTABLE HEAD HALTER

△ FIGURE-OF-EIGHT HEAD COLLAR

BODY HARNESS FOR SMALL-HEADED DOGS

17 PUTTING ON A HEAD HALTER

A large dog that could become difficult to control in public will be more responsive to a head halter.

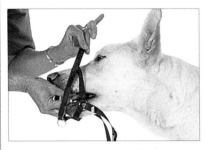

1 Slip a strong, nylon head halter over the dog's mouth, putting your hand under its jaw to hold its head up.

2 Fasten the halter behind the dog's neck. Make sure it is not tight: you should be able to slip two fingers under it.

18 SAFE STEPS TO MUZZLE YOUR DOG

Where the law or common sense about bite prevention dictates, make sure your dog wears a muzzle.

1 Kneel by your dog and strap on the muzzle, starting from under its chin. Pull the straps behind gently and fasten.

2 Make sure the muzzle fits securely, but that it is not too tight. The dog should be able to open its jaws and pant.

19 HANDLING WITH A CHECK CHAIN

When out walking, especially if there are children about, and for boisterous breeds with short attention spans, a check chain or a half-check collar is ideal for sure control.

Dog responds to half-check collar

1 Hold the check chain open in a circle and gently slip it over the dog's head. It should hang loosely around its neck.

HALF-CHECK COLLAR
Pull up on the lead to tighten. This gives firm control over aggression.

2 In the correct position, as shown, it will tighten only when tension is applied. Keep the dog on your left side.

INCORRECT METHOD
If the chain is put on backwards it will cause discomfort and will not loosen.

20 BEDDING DOWN

Set up the dog bed in a busy part of the home, such as a kitchen corner. A bean bag can make a light, soft bed that retains body heat and is easy to wash; or why not consider a chew-proof, plastic basket, with a washable mattress: it is harder wearing and easier to clean than a wicker version.

A SECURE PLACE TO WATCH THE FAMILY

21 PUPPY PEN FOR PEACE OF MIND

It is worth buying a secure puppy pen, with an open top, for a new, untrained dog. Ensure it has:

- Newspaper to soak up accidents.
- Fresh water and a chewy toy.
- A comfortable basket or bean bag.

Always leave fresh water

Puppy can watch house activity

Newspaper for toilet training

Toy for stimulation

HEALTHY FEEDING

22 THE BEST BOWLS

A dog must have its own feeding bowl. For durability, buy your dog a stainless steel bowl, with the bottom rimmed with rubber to prevent sliding. A heavy ceramic bowl can't be knocked over easily, but if it chips or cracks replace it, as bacteria will breed there.

Ceramic bowl

Puppy bowl

Stainless steel bowl

23 HOW MUCH WATER?

Make sure your dog has fresh water available, and replenish to the same level daily. A dog loses water every day in urine, faeces, and through panting. Your dog could suffer from irreversible body dehydration and damage if water is not available for over 48 hours.

Keep the water bowl clean and refill it daily

24 SIMPLE STEPS ON HOW AND WHEN TO FEED

You can give an adult dog, generally over nine months old, their daily food allowance in one meal; or you can split the same amount into two meals a day.

- Small dogs have smaller stomachs and eat less in one meal. Therefore, to help its digestion, feed a small dog on a twice daily basis.
- Puppies need three or more meals a day, reduced to two when they reach six months old. From six to nine months of age you can start to introduce adult dog food.
- For a sick dog, treat it as you would a puppy, giving three small daily meals. Try giving it a gravy broth served in a saucer if it refuses to eat any solid food.
- Pregnant bitches need up to 50 per cent more food. Consult a vet on any special dietary needs.

- Make sure the basic diet includes protein for growth and tissue repair.
- Check for essential fatty acids to give a glossy sheen to a dog's coat.
- Look for carbohydrates in the ingredients, to provide bulk and help your dog's bowel movements.
- Little and often is a good rule for older dogs. Over 12 years of age, food becomes a daily highlight.
- Always be sure to serve your dog's meal at room temperature.
- Never offer stale or spoiled food.
- Never feed processed cat food to your dog: it is too high in protein.
- Do not feed brittle bones, such as chicken, which it might choke on.
- Remove canned or wet food after 10 to 15 minutes, and give a new serving at the next mealtime.
- If your dog refuses to eat for 24 hours, consult your vet.

Daily requirements for normal adult dog

Dog weight/type	Calories needed	Canned food/meal	Semi-moist food	Dry food
Very small:5 kg/11 lb Yorkshire Terrier	210	105 g/4 oz meat 35 g/1 oz meal	70 g/2 oz	60 g/2 oz
Small:10 kg/22 lb Cairn Terrier	590	300 g/11 oz meat 100 g/4 oz meal	190 g/7 oz	170 g/6 oz
Medium:20 kg/44 lb Springer Spaniel	900	450 g/1 lb meat 150 g/5 oz meal	300 g/11 oz	260 g/9 oz
Large:40 kg/88 lb German Shepherd	1,680	850 g/2 lb meat 280 g/10 oz meal	545 g/1¾ oz	480 g/1 lb
Giant:80 kg/176 lb Great Dane	2,800	1.4 kg/3 lb meat 460 g/1 lb meal	900 g/2 lb	900 g/1¾ lb

25 DECIDING ON FRESH FOOD

Meat provides most, but not all, of a dog's daily nutritional needs. However, like humans, dogs cannot live on meat alone, so if you are going to feed your dog fresh food rather than prepared foods, make sure to mix the meat with the correct amount of cereals, vegetables, pasta, and rice to provide all the protein, carbohydrate, fat, vitamins, and minerals it needs for good health. The nutrient content of fresh meat varies considerably, so keeping a consistently balanced diet can be quite difficult.

MEAT AND VEGETABLES
All your dog's nutritional needs are in this dish.

HIGH-FAT MINCED MEAT
A major source of calories, with a high level of fat.

LOW-CALCIUM LIVER
Rich in vitamins A, B₁, high phosphorus, low calcium.

HIGH-CALORIE HEART
High fat content; double the calories of kidney.

LOW-CALORIE CHICKEN
Easily digested and lower in calories than other meats.

LIGHT SCRAMBLED EGG
Non-meat nutrition for very young and recuperating dogs.

ENERGY-GIVING PASTA
Good carbohydrate source, but may need flavouring.

26 VEGETABLES FOR DOGS

Uncooked vegetables (and certain raw fruits) are good sources of vitamins. Dogs are not total meat-eaters and can convert vegetable protein and fat into the nutrients necessary to survive. So choose freshly cooked vegetables, such as carrots, cabbage, and potatoes, as part of a well-balanced diet. If you want to put your dog on a vegetarian diet, consult your vet about how to maintain balanced nutrition.

VITAMIN-RICH MIXED VEGETABLES

27 COMPLETE DRY FOODS

These almost odourless meat and fish pellets have four times as many calories per gram as canned food, so feed in smaller quantities. Some types must be rehydrated with water. Do not confuse these complete meals with snack-based, mainly cereal dog-meals or biscuits.

REHYDRATED

FOR ELDERLY DOG   LOW CALORIE

HIGH ENERGY

STANDARD DRY

28 COMPLETE SEMI-MOIST FOOD

Complete semi-moist food has more than three times the calories of canned food and makes an excellent prepared pet meal. It provides a complete and economical diet and you can give it to your dog by itself or with a cereal filler. It has a high carbohydrate content suitable for working dogs – but not for diabetic dogs. It also tends to have a shorter shelf life than dry or canned food.

SEMI-MOIST MEAL

29 CANNED FOOD CHOICE

Meaty, high-protein, canned foods come in many varieties to suit different dog owners' requirements. The main variety is a meat-in-jelly mix, best given to your dog with an equal volume of cereal filler or crunchy dry food to ensure a good level of calories, carbohydrates, and fat. Some canned foods are prepared for dogs with finicky appetites and can be fed without dry food, still giving a dog enough nutrients.

MEAT-IN-JELLY MIX

MADE-TO-MEASURE PLASTIC LIDS

30 STORING FOOD

Fit a plastic lid on top of a partly used can of dog food, and store in a refrigerator for a maximum of three days. Wash the lids after use, separately from the family cutlery – as you would wash the dog's bowls and serving spoon.

31 VITAMINS & MINERALS

Your dog should get all the vitamins and minerals it requires from either the fresh meat, cereals, vegetables, or prepared pet foods you give it. However, there are certain times when a dog may require supplements to ensure bone growth, good digestion, tissue repair, water balance, and other conditions. These include during pregnancy, puppy growth, and when a dog is recuperating from injury or illness. If your pet is in such a condition, talk to your vet about the level of supplement needed before adding any to its diet.

CALCIUM
Essential for puppies and pregnant and lactating bitches.

VITAMIN TABLETS
Dispense only as directed by your vet.

BONEMEAL
An extra source of calcium: buy it sterilized.

32 BONES OR CHEWS?

Bones for chewing help to supply vital calcium, but if you feed your dog a balanced diet, it will be receiving enough calcium already. Gnawing on bones massages the gums and exercises the jaw muscles. Beef shin or knuckle bones are best since they are less likely to splinter when gnawed or to stick in the mouth. Bones are dangerous for some dogs. Consult a vet before providing them. Chews are an effective and more convenient alternative, with fewer calories.

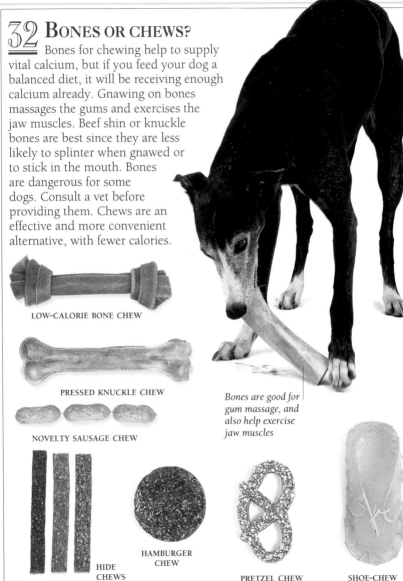

LOW-CALORIE BONE CHEW

PRESSED KNUCKLE CHEW

NOVELTY SAUSAGE CHEW

Bones are good for gum massage, and also help exercise jaw muscles

HIDE CHEWS

HAMBURGER CHEW

PRETZEL CHEW

SHOE-CHEW

33 TITBITS & TREATS

Off-the-shelf biscuits, chunks, and rings make tasty snacks and are useful training rewards. Such treats are high in carbohydrates and fat, which means high calories, so take them into account when considering your dog's daily calorie intake.

BONE-SHAPED BISCUITS

CHEESE FLAVOURED

WHOLEMEAL BISCUIT

MINI MARROWBONE

MIXED FLAVOURS

BACON FLAVOURED

CHICKEN STRIPS

BEEF BONES

BEEF SOFT CHUNKS

SAVOURY RINGS

34 WEIGHT WATCH FOR DOGS

If your dog is less alert than usual, and if you also cannot feel its ribs, you may be overfeeding it, or probably feeding it incorrectly.

- Aim to give your dog only 60 per cent of its normal recommended calorie allowance during dieting.
- Reduce a dog's dry food intake if feeding it a meat and dry food mix.

- Increase the dog's daily exercise.
- Vary the diet from time to time.
- Do not give in to begging for food: this can be an obsession with some dogs, especially if they are bored. Surrendering just reinforces this behaviour and leads to obesity.
- Consult your vet about specially formulated, low-calorie diets.

ESSENTIAL EARLY LEARNING

35 USE A NEWSPAPER

If you have a new adult dog that has not been house-trained, treat it just like a new puppy. Puppies relieve themselves every few hours after eating, drinking, waking, or playing. Train your dog to use newspaper indoors, before moving outside.

1 ▷ Sniffing the ground is the sure, and often the only, sign that your dog wants to relieve itself. You only have a few seconds in which to intervene, so have newspaper ready.

Sniffs to find spot to urinate

2 Quickly pick up the dog and place it on the newspaper. Newspaper is ideal as it is very absorbent. Then keep checking and stand by to encourage it.

3 If you can, keep some of the soiled newspaper to show the puppy its own odour and to encourage it to use that spot again. Praise your puppy afterwards.

36 CRATE-TRAINING ROUTINE

A dog that has been trained from puppyhood to use a crate will see it as a secure haven in a busy area, such as a kitchen. Dogs will not willingly foul their sleeping area, so it is ideal for house-training.
- Leave it in the crate when you are busy. Make sure it has soft bedding, a bowl of fresh water, and a chewy toy.
- Keep a regular check if it wants to relieve itself, especially after it has just eaten or woken up.
- Do not leave your dog in its crate for more than two to three hours at a time during the daytime.
- Keep a newspaper (*see p.28*) in view so the puppy comes to recognize this as its first toilet area.

SAFE AND SECURE "HOME"

37 WHEN TOILET TRAINING FAILS

Your new dog or puppy is bound to have accidents to start with, but never punish it for making a mess in the home. This only makes it more nervous. Nor should you use a crate as a place of discipline: it serves as a home, not a jail, and should be your pet's favourite resting place.

Clean up a messy area with an odour-eliminating disinfectant, because dogs will return to the same smell and defecate there again. Do this quickly as dog droppings are unpleasant and a health hazard. Avoid using ammonia products to clear up because the smell may remind a dog of its own urine.

Wash hands afterwards

Disinfectant kills germs

Wear rubber gloves

38 OUTDOOR TOILET TRAINING

As soon as possible, train your puppy to go to the toilet outside. Start with your garden (where you can remove the faeces and flush it away), then go to a suitable public space with a poop scoop. Keep it on a lead until it relieves itself in a specific spot.

1 ▷ Standing by the door is a sign that a dog wants to relieve itself outside.

2 Train your dog to sniff out a remote spot to urinate on. Luckily, dogs like to relieve themselves in specific places.

3 Use words like "hurry up" as it relieves itself; then praise it. Soon your dog will relieve itself on your "hurry up" command.

39 HOW TO SCOOP POOP

A walk stimulates a dog to defecate, usually within the first ten minutes. Always carry a poop scoop or biodegradable bag, and keep your dog on a lead until it deposits on a suitable spot (give the lead a quick jerk if the site is unacceptable). Afterwards let the dog off the lead. It will soon learn that it has to perform before it can play. Clear up with the poop scoop, or bag, and deposit faeces in a bin.

PURPOSE-MADE POOP SCOOP

40 STOP CHEWING!

Puppies chew out of curiosity about the things around them; older dogs delight in chewing objects, such as shoes, which you would not normally allow. Limit chewing to one or two permissible objects so your pet learns to chew only what you give it.

Apply bitter, non-toxic spray on objects it wants but you don't want it to have

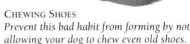

CHEWING SHOES
Prevent this bad habit from forming by not allowing your dog to chew even old shoes.

41 STOP STEALING FOOD!

Dogs instinctively look for food; what we think is rubbish can be tasty to a dog. Train your pet to feed only from its bowl and make sure you leave all food covered.

- Use a firm verbal "leave" command.
- Put the lid firmly on the bin to hide any tempting food morsels.
- Squirt the bin with a bitter-tasting spray to make it unpleasant to the dog.

KEEP FOOD OUT OF SIGHT

ESSENTIAL EARLY LEARNING

Refuse to allow it any titbits from the table

42 STOP BEGGING!

Train your pet to take food only from its bowl, well away from where you eat. Command your dog to "sit", put its bowl on the floor, then say "okay" and allow it to eat.

FIRM COMMAND
Firm body language backs up verbal "sit" command.

Dog makes desire for treat obvious

HOWLS OF BOREDOM
A dog may howl when it is bored or lonely.

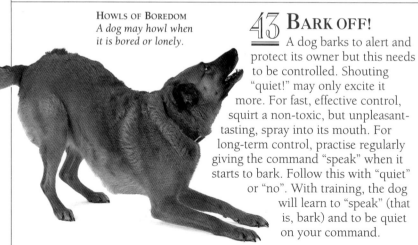

43 BARK OFF!

A dog barks to alert and protect its owner but this needs to be controlled. Shouting "quiet!" may only excite it more. For fast, effective control, squirt a non-toxic, but unpleasant-tasting, spray into its mouth. For long-term control, practise regularly giving the command "speak" when it starts to bark. Follow this with "quiet" or "no". With training, the dog will learn to "speak" (that is, bark) and to be quiet on your command.

GOOD GROOMING

44 SHEDDING HAIRS
Smooth and short-haired coats can shed all year, and require frequent brushing. Curly and wiry coats moult less; they keep growing, and need regular attention.

45 CLIPS & CUTS
Fast-growing coats need to be clipped or cut, while heavy coats require thinning out. Accustom your pet to a routine (and to the sound of clippers), as a young dog.

46 PREPARE TO GROOM
Position your pet on a non-slip mat at a height where you do not have to bend over for grooming, and ensure your scissors, brushes, and combs are ready. Hold the dog with a hand under the belly, and put the thumb of the other hand under its collar.

Hand placed palm down

Anti-slip mat

Grooming kit at the ready

47 TURN YOUR DOG
If you cannot reach over the back of your dog to groom its coat on the other side, turn it. Place the flat of your hand, with the fingers reasonably close, over the hind-leg muscles and bring it around. Keep the palm flat to avoid hurting it.

Dog accepts your hands

48 FACE CLEANING

You should inspect your dog's ears, eyes, and teeth once a week. Breeds with skin folds, like this Shar Pei, need extra attention. Daily or weekly routine grooming sessions help keep your pet's face, skin, coat, and nails healthy, and also provide a regular opportunity for you to reinforce your authority and control. If a dog is difficult, start with giving the "sit" and "stay" commands. End each session with verbal praise and reassuring pats.

COTTON WOOL BALLS

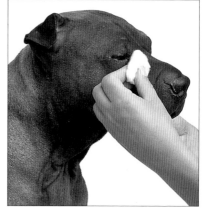

1 Hold the head firmly with one hand; wipe the skin gently around the eye with the other hand, using a fresh piece of damp cotton wool. Remove any mucus.

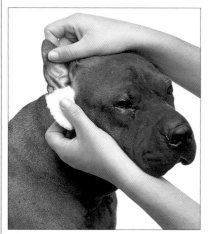

2 With one hand, hold open the ear and gently clean inside the flap with another fresh piece of wet cotton wool. Try to avoid probing deep into the ear.

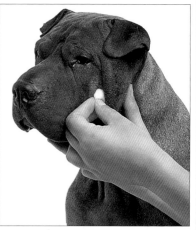

3 Some dogs' facial skin forms natural traps for dirt, debris, and dead skin that harbour bacteria. Clean loose skin regularly with fresh, damp cotton wool.

49 CLEANING TEETH & GUMS

Your dog's teeth should be inspected by a vet at least annually. Once a week, however, you should check that your dog's teeth and gums show no signs of infection. Over 75% of adult dogs require dental attention; the first warning sign is often bad breath caused by bacteria multiplying in food trapped between teeth. If you neglect weekly grooming and an annual vet check-up, removal of teeth may be the only remedy. To prevent tooth decay you can also buy special oral hygiene gels from your local vet. Apply directly as with toothpaste, or mix in with a small amount of food. Do this on average once a week.

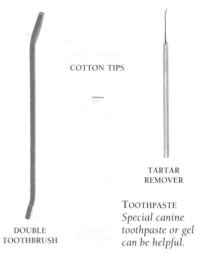

COTTON TIPS

TARTAR REMOVER

TOOTHPASTE
Special canine toothpaste or gel can be helpful.

DOUBLE TOOTHBRUSH

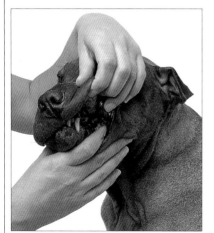

1 Check carefully for dental plaque and hardened tartar. These are caused by bacteria build-up and will lead to bad breath and inflammation of gum tissue.

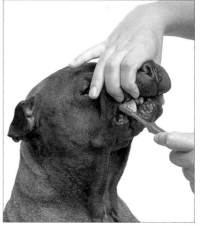

2 Make sure your dog knows you are in command, then gently brush its teeth with a soft toothbrush. Apply special dog toothpaste, gel, or dilute salt water.

50 BATH YOUR DOG

You may need to bath your dog to rid it of skin parasites, to alleviate a skin condition, or just if it rolls in something foul! Apply a medical shampoo recommended by a vet. Rinse well as left-over shampoo may cause needless skin irritation.

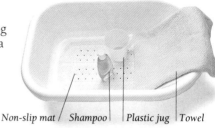

Non-slip mat / *Shampoo* | *Plastic jug* | *Towel*

1 Keep your dog's collar on in the bath to hold the dog and stop it from jumping out. Use a rubber mat in the bath to prevent your dog slipping. You may also want to plug its ears with cotton wool. Hold the collar and pour warm water on its coat.

2 Keeping one hand on the collar, use a special canine shampoo to soap the dog all over, except for its head. Work up a good lather, and massage the skin against the lie of the coat. Rub the shampoo well into its coat to loosen dirt and dead skin.

3 Now, use both hands to lather the dog's head, massaging the hair gently. You will not need to hold on to its collar at this stage. Be extremely careful not to splash the eyes with soapy water, and to avoid getting the lather in your pet's mouth.

4 Rinse and dry the dog's head thoroughly before rinsing the body. It is most likely to shake when its head gets wet, so this will stop it shaking water all over you. Be careful around the ears and eyes, and praise it with encouraging words.

5 Next rinse the rest of its body using clean, warm water. Make sure you remove all the soap from its coat. Keep rinsing until you are sure the coat is shampoo-free. Massage out any excess water.

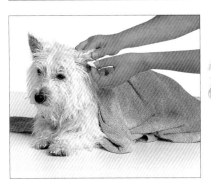

6 When you are sure that you have squeezed out any excess water, dry your dog's coat with a towel and then lift it, wrapped up as much as possible in the towel. Remove the ear plugs and dry the inside of the ears carefully. Always remember to dry well under the collar.

7 Towel-dry the coat thoroughly, or, if your dog has healthy skin, use a hair dryer. Set the dial on warm, not hot, and reassure your pet verbally if it is startled or not used to the loud machine sound. Do not use a hair dryer if it is prone to itchiness, as heat exaggerates this.

51. TRIMMING NAILS

The best time to trim nails is just after a bath, when the nails are softer than usual. Be careful not to trim the pink area lying inside the nail.

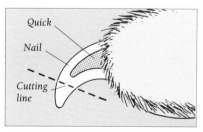

NAIL CLIPPERS

1 △ Spread each of your dog's feet and inspect the area between the toes for dirt and debris. Clean in the recesses with a piece of moistened cotton wool.

2 ◁ Clip your pet's nails carefully using purpose-made canine or "guillotine" nail clippers. Smooth over any rough edges with a nail file or emery board.

52. WHERE TO TRIM

The pink area underneath the nail is living tissue with blood and nerves, and is called the quick, or nail bed. You must avoid cutting this tissue when trimming the nails. Cut diagonally down the nail only a very few millimetres. If in doubt, ask your vet to perform this for you.

Quick

Nail

Cutting line

KEEP THE CUT IN FRONT OF THE PINK AREA

53 GROOMING A SHORT COAT

Short coats need less grooming than long coats, but some are prone to heavy moulting. To control the hair and dandruff, a daily groom may be necessary.

BRISTLE   **SLICKER**   **COMB**

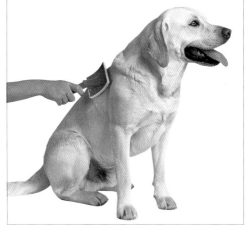

1 Use a slicker brush that is specially designed to remove tangles and prevent matting (short, dense coats matt easily). With firm, long strokes, brush along your pet's body and tail.

2 Next use a bristle brush to remove all dead hair and remaining dirt. Brush the entire coat, including tail and legs.

3 Run a fine comb through the "feathers" on the dog's legs and tail. If there are straggling hairs from the "feathers", trim these with scissors. While grooming, check your pet for parasites and sores.

54 GROOMING A SMOOTH COAT

Smooth-coated dogs, such as Boxers, are the easiest to groom, and look at their peak with a brush and polish once or twice a week. Use conditioner to help soften the hair.

RUBBER BRUSH   CHAMOIS   BRISTLE BRUSH

1 Select a rubber brush, and use this first to loosen any dead hair and surface dirt. Work against the lie of the fur to help you loosen the debris.

2 Next use a bristle brush to remove the dead hair and skin. Make sure you brush the dog's entire coat and do not ignore grooming its tail and legs.

3 Polish your pet's coat briskly with a chamois cloth to bring out the shine. You can also apply a coat conditioner to give your dog's coat a glossy sheen.

55 HAND STRIPPING A WIRY COAT

Dogs with wiry coats must be hand-stripped every three or four months. Pluck dead hair using your thumb and finger, or thumb and stripping knife, in direction of growth.

STANDARD STRIPPING KNIFE

HAIR PLUCKED BETWEEN THUMB AND KNIFE

56 SUCCESS WITH SILKY COATS

Long coats require more care than short coats. Silky coated dogs like Yorkshire Terriers have no downy undercoat, and need extra care when grooming to avoid scratching the skin.

SLICKER COMB SCISSORS BRUSH

1 Use a slicker brush, specially designed to remove any tangles. Gently tease out the matts, taking special care not to pull on your pet's hair and break it.

2 Groom the coat again, using a bristle brush to bring out the shine. At this stage, the brush should move through the coat with very little resistance.

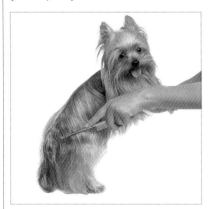

3 Carefully take the long hair on the dog's back and part down either side of the centre using the comb, and then comb each side straight down. You can trim any straggling ends with scissors.

4 Trim carefully around the feet and ears with the scissors. You can trim above the eyes, or tie the hair back with a bow.

Neat and gleaming coat _____

GOOD GROOMING

57 TAKING OUT LONG HAIR TANGLES

Dogs with long coats, such as Rough Collies and Shetland Sheepdogs, also have dense, thick, protective down. If you do not regularly groom your dog's long coat using both a slicker and a bristle brush, it will matt easily, and you will find it difficult to achieve a sleek and tidy coat.

SLICKER   SCISSORS   COMB   PIN BRUSH

1 If you own a long-haired dog, such as a Rough Collie, you must give it a daily thorough groom as well as a regular, but less frequent, trim. Start with a slicker brush and gently untangle your pet's matted hair and knots. Avoid being too vigorous when you brush the coat.

2 Take a pin brush and run through your dog's coat, not too vigorously, so you avoid pulling out the hair. There should be no large tangles left. Long-haired dogs with thick coats can get matts under their legs: take extra care when grooming these areas, where the skin is usually more sensitive.

3 Comb through the hair with a wide-toothed comb, to break up any leftover small tangles. Follow this with a finer comb. Good quality steel, wide-toothed and fine-toothed combs are essential for removing tangles, matts, and debris from thicker, longer hair. Do not use short bristle brushes.

4 Trim your dog's long hair around the feet with a pair of sharp scissors. Remember to trim between the toes, where dirt can become lodged and may cause irritation if not removed. Reduce the risk of dirt becoming embedded between the toes by trimming the hair directly after exercise.

5 Trim around the hocks (the central back joint on the hind legs) and feathers (the long, fine fringe of hairs) with the sharp scissors, so that the hair does not become tangled and collect dirt and debris. You should groom a long-haired dog for at least 15 minutes to make the session effective.

TAKING THE LEAD

58 STARTING YOUR DOG'S TRAINING

Dogs have short attention spans, so keep each training session short, and always end it on a positive, encouraging note. Use verbal praise, physical reassurance, and an instant reward to reinforce initial training.

- Always use a lead to ensure control.
- Sessions to last no more than 15 minutes, twice a day maximum.
- Cancel if you or the dog are tired.
- End each session on a positive note.
- Finish training with a play session.

59 GIVING COMMANDS

You will need to use food rewards at first to reinforce your commands. A hungry dog is alert and ready to respond. Make the treat visible but do not offer your dog any morsel until it carries out a command.

FOOD INDUCED ▷
Effective reward for hungry dog.

No offer of food, but verbal praise

Dog sits to verbal command only

Dog sits on command for reward

△ WORD ENFORCED
Reduce snacks gradually, so the dog reacts solely to your body language and verbal praise.

60 COMMAND YOUR DOG TO SIT

The first and generally easiest commands to teach your dog are to "sit" and "come" on command.

- Practise control first with a lead.
- Start sessions with a food reward.
- Aim to make it sit by words alone.

Dog responds to food held in front of middle of body

Food held directly above dog's head

1 Face the dog, move away with the lead in your left hand and treat in your right. Say "come" and show it the treat.

2 As it reaches you, move your right hand up and over its head. It will bend its hind legs as it keeps an eye on the food.

3 Give the command "sit" when you see it about to sit. Then practise again, and from the side. Reduce the treat each time.

61 REFUSING TO SIT

Making your new dog or puppy learn to sit down will take many practice sessions. If it refuses to sit even with a treat, kneel down and hold its collar with your right hand. Tuck its hindquarters under with your left hand and give the command "sit" as you do this. Reward the dog with praise and a treat. Repeat the step, giving just praise alone, until it responds to this.

Fingers kept together in the tuck, to avoid hurting the dog

62 WAIT & COME COMMAND

Making your dog wait, and then come to you when you call it, is known as recall training. An untrained dog is bound to follow you at first, so take it back and repeat the command (*see step 1*).

1 ◁ Place your dog in the sit position and give the command "sit-wait". Avoid the word "stay", which it might confuse with the "stay till I return" command.

2 ▷ Draw the length of the lead away from your dog, face the dog, show a food reward, and call its name, adding the command "come".

Dog moves towards you, and the treat

Dog sees food treat in right hand

4 ▽ Now practise the commands over a greater distance, with your dog on a long line. Use a toy reward that your dog can see from a distance, rather than offering a food morsel.

Long line is slack, but can be pulled to ensure compliance

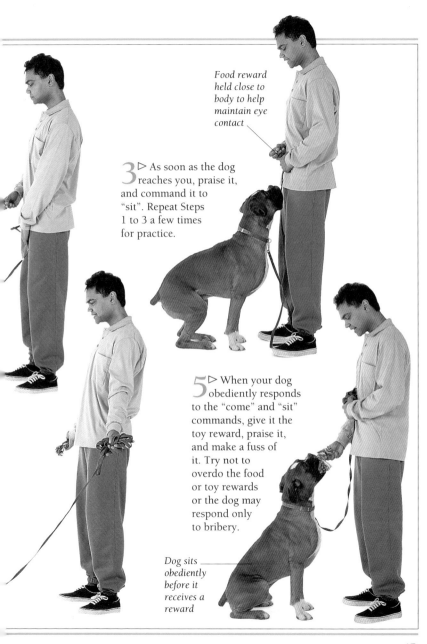

Food reward held close to body to help maintain eye contact

3 ▷ As soon as the dog reaches you, praise it, and command it to "sit". Repeat Steps 1 to 3 a few times for practice.

5 ▷ When your dog obediently responds to the "come" and "sit" commands, give it the toy reward, praise it, and make a fuss of it. Try not to overdo the food or toy rewards or the dog may respond only to bribery.

Dog sits obediently before it receives a reward

63 COMMAND TO LIE DOWN

This command teaches the dog that you are in control; it is a good command to use when there are a lot of distractions. There are two lying positions: the "sphinx", where the hind legs tuck under the body, and "flat", where the hips are rolled and the legs are on one side. Either position is natural.

End of lead held secure under knees

1 Command the dog to "sit"; kneel beside it and hold its collar to restrain. Keep a treat in the other hand.

Food held in clenched fist to stop dog from snatching

2 Place the treat on the dog's nose and move it downwards. As the dog sniffs the treat, move the treat forwards in front of its nose and body.

Dog moves down to keep in touch with the treat

3 As you move the treat forwards the dog should naturally start to stretch forwards and lie down. Praise and reward it. Repeat the exercise until it responds to your words without a treat.

64 IF DOG WON'T LIE DOWN

With any early training, be it on or off the lead, expect to do quite a few practice runs, particularly with a puppy. If, after several practices, your dog still refuses to lie down, encourage it first into a begging position. Kneel down with the dog on your left side. Place your right palm under the dog's right foreleg, and then your left palm under its left foreleg. Now, raise it into a begging position. Gently lower the dog into either the "sphinx" or "flat" lying position. Keep calling its name and praising it all the time.

Gently hold the dog's legs. Do not grip them

1 To achieve a begging position, prior to lying-down, kneel beside the dog and position your hands comfortably, one under each of its forelegs. Reassure it with praise, and lower the dog into the lying position.

2 Ease it to the ground by gently pressing on its body and by pulling its legs forwards. Keep the pressure on its shoulders for a few seconds once it lies down. Praise it, and on release say "okay". If it still jumps up, stop the praise, put it back in position and start again.

Keep fingers together over dog's shoulder muscles

65 HOW TO PRAISE

A dog needs to be shown and reassured that it is responding correctly to commands. Food titbits, toys, stroking its body, and constant verbal praise help you to reinforce this. If, in training, your dog does exactly what you want, do not hesitate to make a fuss of it.

△ COMFORTING CONTACT
Praise your dog by giving it long strokes along its body. Use the flat of your palm to make even strokes.

◁ HAND-HELD TASTY TREATS
Food held above a dog's nose will attract its attention quickly, especially if the dog is hungry.

66 SENSIBLE REWARDS

After a few training runs you will soon learn which snack or toy your dog responds to. Strap on a waist bag during training sessions so you can pull out titbits or toys without interrupting its learning.

RING TOY

DRIED FOOD

BISCUITS

CHEW STICKS

THROW BALL   BONE TOY

67 PULLING ON THE LEAD

Pulling on the lead is the most common problem faced by dog owners. The remedy is to re-train (*see pp.44–9*) and command to heel (*see pp.52–5*). Don't try to match your strength against the dog as this may only incite it to pull even more.

EXCITED LEAD PULLING

1 ◁ Walk the dog on your left side, and hold the lead in both hands. As it pulls, slide your left hand down the lead and pull firmly.

Hands pulls back once, firmly

Light jerks on lead bring dog into position

Give a small food reward each time it heels and sits without pulling

2 △ With your dog in the correct heel position, command it to sit. Start to walk again. Now try walking to heel (*see pp.52–3*).

3 ◁ Repeat the "heel" and "sit" procedure each time the dog pulls forward. When it starts to walk quietly to heel without pulling, reward it with a food treat and try it again.

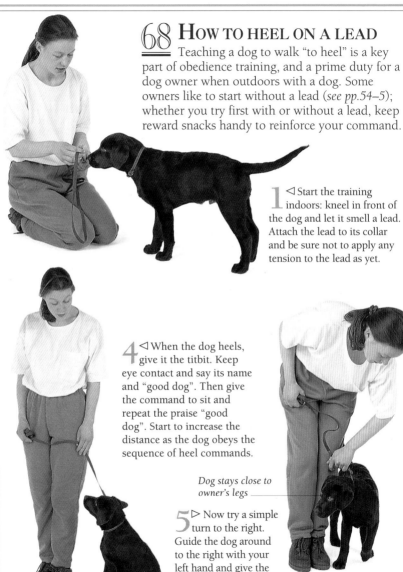

68 HOW TO HEEL ON A LEAD

Teaching a dog to walk "to heel" is a key part of obedience training, and a prime duty for a dog owner when outdoors with a dog. Some owners like to start without a lead (*see pp.54–5*); whether you try first with or without a lead, keep reward snacks handy to reinforce your command.

1 ◁ Start the training indoors: kneel in front of the dog and let it smell a lead. Attach the lead to its collar and be sure not to apply any tension to the lead as yet.

4 ◁ When the dog heels, give it the titbit. Keep eye contact and say its name and "good dog". Then give the command to sit and repeat the praise "good dog". Start to increase the distance as the dog obeys the sequence of heel commands.

Dog stays close to owner's legs

5 ▷ Now try a simple turn to the right. Guide the dog around to the right with your left hand and give the command "heel".

*Left hand
ready to
slide down
lead to collar*

2 ◁ Now give the
"sit" command.
With the dog on
your left side, hold
the lead and a food
reward in your right
hand, with no
tension on the collar.
Hold the slack in
your left hand.

*Lead given
a quick jerk*

3 △ Begin to walk with
the dog beside you,
then give the command
"heel". Pull back gently
on the lead or collar if
the dog surges forwards.

6 ▷ To make a left
turn, increase your
own speed and hold a
treat in front of the dog's
nose to slow it down.
Keep the dog close to
your left leg, and give
the command "steady"
to help slow it down.

*Owner holds
dog back by
its collar*

*Dog is kept
close to your
legs at all
times*

69 HEEL WITHOUT A LEAD

When out walking with your dog it must always be under control. Training a dog to heel with a lead will help you ensure that control, although it is also a delight to have your pet walking obediently by your side without a lead. Most dogs, especially from a young age, will naturally follow their owner, especially if there is the extra lure of a treat in sight. Keep food treats handy and make training sessions enjoyable, short, and frequent; no more than 15 minutes, up to four times a day. Practise in a quiet area, away from crowds if possible.

Keeping eye contact is crucial

1 △ Keep the dog on your left side and hold its collar with your left hand. Attract its attention by calling its name and showing it the tasty titbit.

Owner repeats the "heel" command and says "good dog" to encourage it

Arm draws dog to the right, encouraging a turn

4 ▷ To encourage a right turn, bend your knees and hold the food near to the dog's nose. Make the right turn repeating the "heel" command as you do this. The dog will have to speed up to walk around you.

Dog's head follows the treat intently

Arm prevents dog surging forwards

Scent of food keeps dog on the move

2 △ Walk in a straight line with the dog following the food reward. Give the command "heel". Keep your left hand low, and bend downwards, ready to grasp the dog's collar.

3 △ Give the command "wait", and kneel to your dog's right side. Hold the snack low to discourage any jumping. Place your left hand, palm down, under its body, near to its hind legs, to prevent the dog from moving forwards.

Dog slows down as it receives reward

5 ▷ To make a left turn, use your left hand to guide the dog round by its collar while giving the command "steady". Hold a food reward low down and move your right hand to the left. The dog should follow the reward. Try several practice walks.

70 MEETING CHILDREN

Children are more at risk from bites because they are smaller and less imposing than adults. Explain to any child that wants to stroke your dog that some dogs can be unfriendly and that they must never rush up, shout, or pat the dog on its head. The dog should be introduced to children only in the presence, and under the supervision, of an adult. Allow the child to stroke the dog from the side, not the front. Praise the dog for its good behaviour, but be ready to restrain it if it snaps or growls.

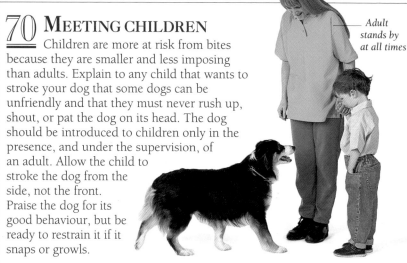

Adult stands by at all times

71 MEETING OTHER DOGS

Be cautious when your dog encounters another dog. Most dogs do get on with each other, but male territorial traits often lead to fights. Fighting is more likely between dogs of the same sex, size, and age. Avoid lead tension, and praise your dog for just sniffing other dogs and not showing any signs of aggression.

Taut lead encourages aggression

72 UNSAVOURY EATING HABITS

Animal droppings can appear nourishing to dogs, and scavenging around horse droppings and the like is natural for some dogs such as the Golden Retriever. If you see your dog behaving in this way, first give the command "no". If it picks up the "droppings" say "drop". Surprise it with a water pistol or distract it with a toy to back up your command. A few dogs will eat their own (or even another dog's) droppings. To help prevent this bad habit recurring, taint a recently passed stool with a spicy, peppery sauce.

Sauce is unpleasant to the dog

73 A FIRM HAND

To reinforce your verbal commands, hand signals, and body language generally, it's useful to have a few back-ups to make sure your dog understands it is behaving badly or not responding to your authority. Plant sprays, water pistols, whistles, alarms, and toys are useful distractions to help you discipline a dog and say "no" or "stop it". Do not physically punish a dog for unwanted behaviour. A dominant stance, stern words, and a squirt or whistle will suffice.

PLANT SPRAY

WATER PISTOL

ALARM

DISTRACTING TOY

PLAY TIME & EXERCISE

74 CHOOSE A CHEWY TOY

Dogs enjoy chewing, chasing, and pulling, so make sure they play or exercise with a toy that you choose, rather than with a household item they fancy. A chewy bone exercises the jaws, while pulls are ideal for tug-of-war games. Balls and frisbees are fun for a dog to chase and retrieve.

RUBBER BALL

NYLON BONE

DOG PULL

75 SUITABLE TOYS

Purpose-made toys are designed to be safe and fun for dogs. Restrict the use of any toy to prevent possessiveness in your dog.

- Avoid balls or toys that could be easily destroyed and swallowed.
- Do not give old shoes or clothes. It will assume it can chew new ones.

76 MAKE A CHEWY TOY

Insert cheese spread into hollow bone

A good alternative to ready-made toys is to get a hollow bone, make sure it is sterilized, and then insert cheese spread or paste into its core. Show the bone to your dog and tell it there is food inside, then place it on the floor. This is an ideal "home alone" toy, and your dog will get plenty of chewing practice trying to reach the food.

HOLLOW BONE

77 PLAY BALL & FRISBEE

Chasing after a skimming frisbee or a bouncing ball makes terrific exercise and an exciting outdoor game for your dog. Ensure that you have plenty of unrestricted space to allow as much exercise for your dog as possible. "Catch and retrieve" games are an excellent way to test your dog's reactions and obedience, channel its natural jumping instincts, reduce destructive activity, and help you to assert your authority.

CATCH AND RETRIEVE GAME

PLASTIC FRISBEE

78 TRY TUG-OF-WAR

Bored or inactive dogs are prone to bursts of destructive behaviour. A tug-of-war game with a pull toy helps channel that energy into positive exercise. Make sure that you always win, otherwise your dog will believe that it is dominant over you.

DROP BEFORE YOU TUG
Only play tug-of-war after your dog has learnt how to drop an object on your command.

KNOTTED ROPE TUG TOY

79 EXERCISE DAILY

Once your dog has learnt obedience training, you should take it out at least once a day for exercise on the lead, and let it off the lead to run in a permitted place. Take a ball or frisbee so you can encourage vigorous exercise in a controllable space and a short time.

△ **ON THE LEAD**
An extendible lead allows safe exercise, when other dogs are about.

◁ **OFF THE LEAD**
Allow vigorous exercise at least once a day, as well as frequent walks.

80 JOG THE DOG

Training your dog to run to heel makes exercise rewarding and fun for you and your pet. If running in urban areas or along roads, take care and adhere to the highway code. If you are exercising in the countryside, be sure your dog does not chase farm animals or run on cultivated land. This is when the walking-to-heel command is essential. If you are in doubt about your dog's obedience, it is best to keep it on a lead when you go out jogging.

Ensure the dog stays close by your side

TRAVEL & HOLIDAYS

81 TAKE A TRAVEL BOX

For air or car journeys, crate-trained dogs could go in their crate, if manageable. Otherwise you need a purpose-made travelling box for small dogs. The box (*left*) has a carrying handle, locking catch, ventilation slits, rounded corners for easy cleaning, and plenty of room.

TRAVELLING PET BOX

82 INSTALL A CAR GRILLE

You can buy special safety grilles that restrict dogs to the back of an estate car or a hatchback. This prevents the dog hurtling forward if you should have to stop suddenly, and helps to keep the upholstery in the rest of the car clean.

CAR SAFETY GRILLE

83 SAFETY BELTS FOR DOGS

You can have special seatbelts fitted for dogs that will greatly reduce the risk of your pet being injured in a car accident. A seatbelt is especially useful if you have a car for which a grille is not suitable. The other advantage of a seatbelt is that it prevents the dog distracting you while you are driving. As an alternative, you could tie its lead, attached to its collar, onto a seatbelt anchor. This will also prevent excess movement in its seat.

DOG SEATBELT

COVER THE SEAT

84 CAR TRIPS TIPS

Take your dog on frequent, short trips to get it used to the car.
- Avoid feeding it before a journey.
- Cover the upholstery and floor with old newspapers or towels.
- Use a blind for hot, sunny days.
- Always take a large, plastic water container to quench a dog's thirst.
- Stop every two to three hours so your dog can have a good drink, take some exercise, and relieve itself.

85 STOP OVER-HEATING

Dogs cannot lose heat by sweating: all they can do is pant. They will suffer from heatstroke and can die quickly from over-heating. In summer or winter, a hot car is a death trap for dogs, so never leave a car unattended in warm weather, even in the shade with a window just open, or with the heater running. Use a car sun-blind to block out the sun. An obscured view also helps to calm excitable dogs.

SUNBLIND ON CAR WINDOW

APPLY COLD WATER FAST

86 IF IT OVER-HEATS

Panting, salivation, and later collapse are the surest signs that a dog is over-heated. Remove it from the hot spot immediately. Clear its mouth of saliva to ease breathing, and sponge the face with cool water. If possible, wrap the dog's body in a wet, but not ice-cold, towel. Pour cold water over the towel to prevent further warming. Give it a drink.

87 WATER SAFETY

If you are taking your dog on a boating holiday on the sea, a lake, or any open stretch of water a long way from shore, put a life jacket on it. Dogs can be excellent swimmers over short distances, but they can drown from exhaustion if they have to swim a long way. A life jacket will help the animal to stay buoyant if it falls in, while awaiting rescue.

Dog life jacket helps it to float

88 HIKING HINT

If you are going on a lengthy hike or trek, you could buy special saddlebags, which a dog will get used to carrying over long distances. The dog backpack can carry your pet's dish, food, and utensils. It is comfortable and has fasteners to secure it. Your dog must be physically fit before you embark on such a trek.

BACKPACK

89 RABIES RISKS

Few countries are rabies-free and those that are consist mainly of islands and peninsulas. Rabies is the most dangerous zoonosis, that is, a disease that can be transmitted from animal to animal, including man. Foxes are common carriers and the virus is transmitted in saliva through bites. Personality change as well as excessive salivation are the warning signs. All dogs should be vaccinated against rabies in those countries where the disease occurs. In rabies-infected areas, humans at risk from dog bites should also be vaccinated.

90 QUARANTINE

If you are bringing a dog to a rabies-free country, you may have to put your pet into special quarantined premises for many months. You must check this carefully well before embarking. Alternatively, you may be asked to prove that your dog was effectively vaccinated against rabies at least four months before your arrival. The costs mount up because approved quarantine premises are expensive and you also have to pay for port or airport carriage, airline handling, transport and veterinary insurance, and rabies vaccinations.

HEALTH CHECKS

91 GOOD HEALTH

You can do your own regular pet health check-up once a month (as shown here), but you should also book your dog for a once-yearly medical examination with your vet.

TEETH AND GUMS
Check for bad breath, dribbling saliva, inflamed gums, and loose or broken teeth.

EYE WATCH
Look for bloodshot eyes, and squinting.

ANAL AREA
Watch out for worms in faeces, white grains on rear, or persistent diarrhoea.

SKIN COMPLAINTS
Be aware of persistent scratching, sudden chewing or licking, redness, and increased hair loss.

SURE SIGNS OF CANINE HEALTH
Healthy dogs are vibrant and alert, though happy to lie down for much of the day.

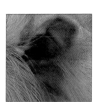

EAR INFECTIONS
Check for head shaking, and ears for discharge of the ear canal, and swelling of the ear flap. A failure to respond to commands may be a sign of deafness.

92 FLEAS

Fleas live in carpets and upholstered chairs and only hop onto dogs for a meal. Look for sooty, black specks in its coat and bed. Spray or powder coat with insecticide, and vacuum bedding area.

ADULT FLEA
A biological spray on a dog's bedding will prevent flea eggs from hatching.

93 MITES & TICKS

Parasites cause scratching, rashes, sores, and swellings. If your pet has mites or ticks, bath it with insecticidal shampoo, and wash its bed. For ticks, dab with surgical spirit, and remove with tweezers, twisting the mouthpiece free.

MITE   TICK   LOUSE

PAWS AND PADS
Inspect the paws for cut or burnt pads, and broken or damaged nails.

94 WORM CHECK

Regular worming of your dog should control most internal parasites. Some worms require special medicines, but your vet will diagnose this and advise on the more severe infestations.

△ **TAPEWORM**
Watch for rice-like eggs around anus or moving in faeces.

◁ **ROUNDWORM**
An earthworm-like parasite visible in the faeces as off-white.

95 FIRST AID KIT

All dog owners would be advised to have a basic first aid kit, the contents of which (*see right*) should assist in reducing a dog's pain and distress, as well as help to prevent the situation worsening while you contact the vet.

TAPE

GAUZE

STRONG HANDY BOX

SCISSORS

COTTON WOOL

DISINFECTANT

MUZZLE

96 BITE TREATMENT

The neck, face, ears, and chest are the body parts where dogs most commonly bite each other. If your dog has been in a fight, allow time for it to calm down before you examine it. Canine teeth make clean bites, so look for soft-tissue damage under the skin. A deep wound will probably have to be treated by a vet. (The safest way to separate fighting dogs is to pour water on them from a bucket or spray with a hosepipe.)

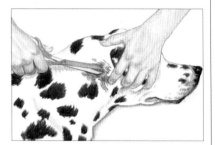

1 If the skin is punctured, you must go to a vet for antibiotics. But first clip the fur away from the wound: fur in the wound can lead to trapped infection.

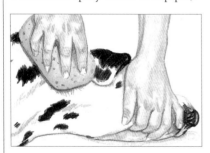

2 Carefully bathe the infected region with warm water and a gentle skin disinfectant. Apply water-soluble jelly to prevent more hair entering the wound.

3 If the dog's skin is lacerated rather than punctured, apply an antiseptic cream to the affected area. Expect some bruising to become visible later on.

97 STING RELIEF

Wasp, hornet, and bee stings are common and cause pain and swelling. The usual sites for these stings are the face and mouth. Like humans, some dogs can be allergic to stings and react badly. If there is acute swelling to the mouth and throat, urgent vet care will be needed.

DRAW OUT A BEE STING WITH TWEEZERS

98 GIVING TABLETS

Some dogs can be devious about keeping pills in their mouths, and spitting them out later. If your pet does this, a good counter-trick is to try hiding the tablet in a chunk of meat, or a piece of bread, or even coat the pill in melted chocolate.

1 △ Go to your dog; do not ask it to come to you. With one hand, open its mouth gently, and with the other drop the tablet well down the tongue.

2 ▷ Hold the dog's mouth firmly closed and hold its head up slightly. Stroke its throat and wait for it to swallow and lick its lips. Then praise it for swallowing.

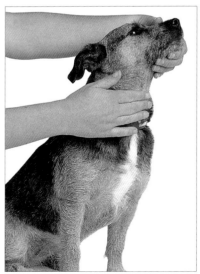

99 MUZZLE & RESTRAIN A HURT DOG

There are, sadly, times when you may have to improvise a muzzle for your dog (if you do not own a muzzle or there is not one to hand). If your dog is hit by a vehicle, it will be in great pain and liable to bite, so you should fit an improvised muzzle before you attempt to examine it or move it to a safer place.

Wrap a bandage or scarf around its nose, knot it under the lower jaw once, and then again behind its neck. Now assess its injuries and get medical help. Once at the veterinary surgery, if the dog is frightened it is always safer for you as the handler, or for a nurse, to muzzle your dog. The best *ad hoc* muzzle is a bandage from your first aid kit (*see p.66*).

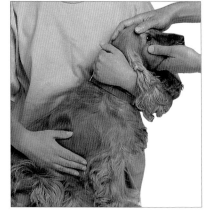

1 During a vet's examination, it is best if you, or a nurse, can hold and give reassuring words to the dog. This should be all the restraining a dog needs.

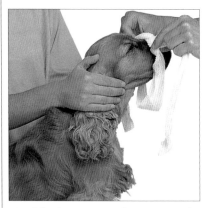

2 If the dog is in great distress, it is safer for a handler to muzzle it. In that case make a wide loop in a bandage and slip it over the dog's nose with the knot on top.

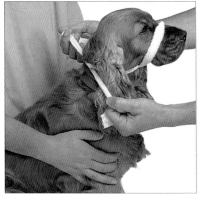

3 Revolve the knot under the dog's lower jaw. Make another loop under the jaw to behind the dog's neck and knot that firmly. (A scarf or tie will do.)

100 STRETCHER FOR AN INJURED DOG

If your dog is in a traffic accident, do not panic. Use a blanket or coat as a stretcher to remove it carefully from the source of danger.

- Muzzle it with a scarf or bandage.
- Look for bleeding, distorted limbs.
- Do not handle a fractured limb.
- Get someone to help you lift it.

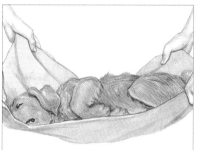

1 Once you have checked the dog's condition, try to get someone to help you to support its weight and lift it onto a blanket or coat. Avoid touching injuries.

2 Lift very gently and carry it to a car to go to the vet. If on your own, place the coat along the dog's back and drag it by the neck and hips onto the stretcher.

101 WHEN TO VISIT THE VET

Every dog-owner must take his or her pet to a vet for a medical check-up at least once a year. If the animal is in an accident, even with no obvious injury or bleeding, take it at once for urgent veterinary help. All vets are linked to a 24-hour emergency service. It may have internal injuries or fractures, which only a professional can diagnose. Visit the surgery also:

- For expert dietary assistance.
- For the best breeding advice.
- If your dog staggers or falls over.
- If blood is present or it is vomiting.
- If in acute pain/abnormal swelling.
- If choking or pawing at the mouth.

Using a stethoscope to check breathing

INDEX

ACKNOWLEDGMENTS

Dorling Kindersley would like to thank Hilary Bird for
compiling the index, Ann Kay for proof-reading, Murdo Culver for
design assistance, and Mark Bracey for computer assistance.

Photography
KEY: t *top*; b *bottom*; c *centre*; l *left*; r *right*; tl *top left;*
tr *top right;* bl *bottom left;*
All photographs by Andy Crawford, Steve Gorton, Tim Ridley,
except for: Jane Burton 12–13, 15t, 72; Guide Dogs for the Blind
Association 9tl; Dave King 3, 7, 8bl, 11, 61b; Tracy Morgan 10t;
Stephen Oliver 21t, 24b; Steve Shott 1, 29b, 30b, 66t; David Ward
8tr, 9b, 10b, 21b, 56b, 60tl; Jerry Young 14 bl.

Illustrations
Rowan Clifford 66, 67, 69; Chris Forsey 63, 65; Janos Marffy 38.